MY OWN RHYTHM

an approach to haiku

MY OWN RHYTHM
an approach to haiku by Ann Atwood

CHARLES SCRIBNER'S SONS, NEW YORK

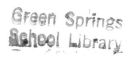

To Jane and Steve. . . . Yes,
in sight there is music, in sound
a luminous silence.

Bashô, Issa and Buson. These were the three great masters
of Japanese haiku, each seeking in the light and movement
of the universe the pulse of his own rhythm.

Their three-line poems reflect intervals of intense
awareness often called "haiku-moments." And though the
sum of oneself is involved in such an experience,
Buson interpreted these moments most often through his mind,
Issa through his heart, and Bashô through his spirit.

Bashô was born of the warrior class, and as a lad was sent to the house of a nobleman where he learned to read and write haiku. Haiku had been part of the Japanese culture for hundreds of years but had deteriorated into little more than a game of words by the seventeenth century, when Bashô raised it to the level of art.

He was an esteemed poet and teacher, and founded his own school of haiku. But comfort and success were not fulfillment to Bashô and he withdrew more and more into silence and solitude.

After studying the philosophy of Zen he denounced even the shelter of his small hut and became a wanderer, a follower of the seasons. He saw beyond the transience of dawn and dusk, summer and winter, a permanence which led him further and further into a union with nature. His joy was the exuberance of spring, and his loneliness was the loneliness of autumn.

He did not insulate himself from "the first winter rain," but chose instead to travel in the company of clouds, glimpsing in the play of the elements what he described as "the hidden glimmering" within all things.

THE SPIRIT OF BASHÔ

The first winter rain,
And my name shall be called,
"Traveller."
BASHÔ

The fawn
Was brought up,
Trodden on by the fowls.

ISSA

Bashô's follower, Issa, had neither the acceptance of the philosopher Bashô nor the detachment of the observer Buson. His was the sensitive nature of the fawn born into a world against which he had few defenses.

An outcast from earliest childhood, Issa was often hungry and alone. He seems to have been destined to a life of poverty, illness, and tragedy. He wrote this famous haiku at the death of one of his children, all five of which he lost:

This dewdrop world—
It may be a dewdrop,
And yet—and yet—

(And yet who can endure the wounds that it inflicts?)

But Issa's strength was in his gentleness. He understood the struggles of the weak, and often showed his rebellion against all class distinction by dressing even more poorly than was necessary. To him all earth's creatures were fellow-travelers, and none escaped his tenderness. He endowed insects and birds and animals with his own humanness.

Though his haiku were often criticized as being too personal and emotional, it was Issa's empathy with every aspect of creation which made him the most loved of all the haiku poets.

Buson was a poet, an artist, and a passionate observer. Little is known of the circumstances surrounding his life, but his poetry reveals a versatile mind which translated a steady flow of quicksilver impressions into fresh and vivid haiku. People moving about in the landscape, or appearing suddenly out of the mist were seen as figures in paintings.

Buson was a master at transforming all sensations into images.

In his haiku "The winter storm," he has made sound visible. We not only hear the voice of the water but we *see* it as well. For though his poems appeal to each of the senses, Buson is irrevocably an artist, keenly focused on the sense of sight.

In his writing he compares and implies, describing the subject perfectly and at the same time letting it suggest something other than itself. In this way he encourages the reader to use his memory and imagination and through the association of ideas to add his own overtones to the haiku.

THE MIND OF BUSON

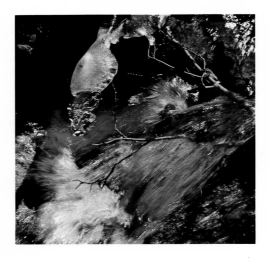

The winter storm,
The voice of the rushing water,
Torn by the rocks.
BUSON

Imagination, emotion, and insight: these are the messengers which bring us knowledge not only of the nature of our environment but of our own natures as well.

A rock in a tide pool is gently washed by a wave. Buson, the artist, would have caught the patterns and colors of the rock in that transparent interval when the water was still.

Issa, the humanist, would have felt the surge
of the wave engulfing the small island.

Bashô, the mystic, would have contemplated
the light which illumined the whole.

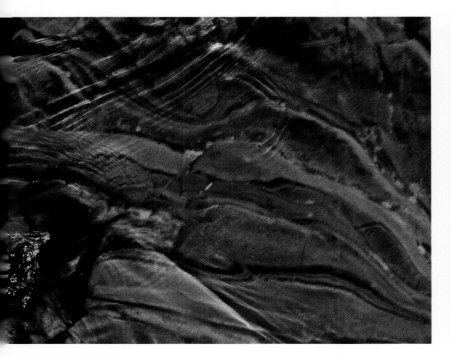

We all think, we all feel, we all aspire.
Through imagining, through feeling, through
intuition, we may enter that state of mind
which is the haiku moment.

This is to become increasingly conscious
of order and design in the world
which surrounds us;

to feel joy and compassion in the company
of every creature who is born of earth,
and whose journey is our journey;

and to listen with quiet attention until we
move to the poetry and music of the universe,
each in his own rhythm.

Knighted by the sun's
bright sword: the boy on horseback
armored in rainbows.

A stairway of light,
the sun's flaming footsteps
halting my journey.

Luminous silence . . .
only color filling the space
between night and day.

Spring on the river—
The island-nest of the swans
floating in flowers.

Spring in the river—
The tips of water grasses
Dripping with diamonds.

A reckless morning . . .
the mother warning her foal,
the nudge of the wind!

So slowly you come
small-snail. . . . To you, how far
is the length of my thumb!

As still as a flower,
yet unlike the flower: the cat
thinking his own thoughts.

The straight strokes of reeds
on the silk summer water.
The rightness of things!

From the dark canoe
slipping home at dusk, the faint
sound of dipping wings.

An ocean of clouds.
Rowing home at evening,
the hurrying gulls.

All day the kite pinned
to the rock has clutched at the sky.
Now, the slackening wind.

The tree after Christmas
facing an incoming tide.
The crying of birds!

*Mingled with the wild
rustling sound of the branches,
the shout of the child!*

Clouds shadow the stream—
a sunburst! and at my feet,
this sudden shining.

Staring at the field
set afire by autumn, the
wide grey eyes of the shed.

The trees' reflection—
a watercolor. The wind
prefers tapestry.

Primitive paintings . . .
the wars, the scars, the glory on
the walls of the shell.

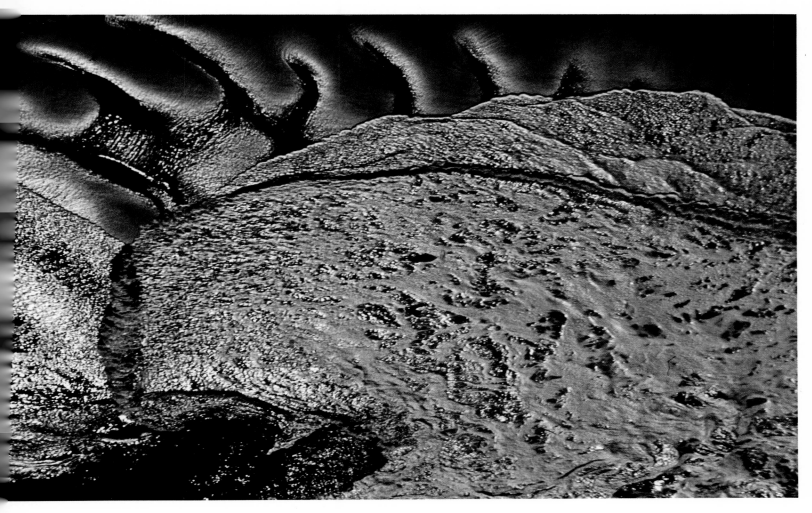

The moon almost full,
the pull in the silver tide,
the sea fanning out . . .

. . . the sea fanning out
and folding in upon itself.
My own rhythm!